FINDING OUT ABOUT HOLIDAYS

Presidents' Day

Honoring the Birthdays of Washington and Lincoln

Mary Dodson Wade

Enslow Publishers, Inc.

40 Industrial Road	PO Box 38
Box 398	Aldershot
Berkeley Heights, NJ 07922	Hants GU12 6BP
USA	UK

http://www.enslow.com

For Ruby and Frank, who care about this country.

Library of Congress Cataloging-in-Publication Data

Wade, Mary Dodson.
  Presidents' Day : honoring the birthdays of Washington and Lincoln /Mary Dodson Wade.
    p. cm. — (Finding out about holidays)
  Summary: Describes the history of the observation of Presidents' Day and provides information on the two presidents
who are honored on this holiday.
  Includes bibliographical references and index.
  ISBN 0-7660-2234-X
  1. Presidents' Day—Juvenile literature. 2. Washington, George, 1732–1799—Juvenile literature. 3. Lincoln, Abraham,
1809–1865—Juvenile literature. 4. Presidents—United States—Juvenile literature. [1. Presidents' Day. 2. Washington, George,
1732–1799. 3. Lincoln, Abraham, 1809–1865. 4. Holidays.] I. Title. II. Series.
    E176.8.W33 2004
    394.261—dc21

                                                                                    2003008758

Printed in the United States of America

10 9 8 7 6 5 4 3 2 1

To Our Readers:

We have done our best to make sure that all Internet Addresses in this book were active and appropriate when we went to press.
However, the author and publisher have no control over and assume no liability for the material available on those Internet sites
or on other Web sites they may link to. Any comments or suggestions can be sent by e-mail to comments@enslow.com or to the
address on the back cover.

Illustration Credits: © Clipart.com, pp. iii (both), 5, 10, 32; © Artville, LLC. , pp. 6, 9; © Corel Corporation, pp. i (left), 8, 10,
13, 15, 20, 21, 34, 35, 38, 40, 44, 46, 47, 48; Cathy Tardosky, pp. 42, 43: Courtesy Benjamin H. Walker, Reproduced from the
Dictionary of American Portraits, published by Dover Publications, Inc., in 1967, p. 11(right); Courtesy New-York Historical
Society, Reproduced from the *Dictionary of American Portraits*, published by Dover Publications, Inc., in 1967, p. 37; Engraving
by Alexander H. Ritchie., Reproduced from the *Dictionary of American Portraits*, published by Dover Publications, Inc., in 1967,
p. 39 (top);Engraving by Henry B. Hall, Jr., Reproduced from the *Dictionary of American Portraits*, published by Dover
Publications, Inc., in 1967, p. 11(left); Enslow Publishers, Inc., pp. 25, 28; © Hemera Technologies, Inc., 1997-2001, pp. ii, 11;
Kim Widenor, p. 30; Library of Congress, pp. i, 7, 11, 12, 14, 16, 17, 18,19, 23, 24, 26, 27, 31, 33, 36, 39 (middle); Painting, First
at Vicksburg, Charles McBarron, Courtesy of the National Museum of the U.S.Army, Army Art Collection, p. 29; Ronald Reagan
Library, 39 (bottom); United States Air Force photo by Staff Sgt. Reynaldo Ramon, p. 4

Cover Photos: © Corel Corporation, background, inset: top, middle; Library of Congress, inset: bottom

CONTENTS

Washington, D.C. is the capital of our country. It is named for George Washington, the first president of the United States. This is the Capitol building in Washington, D.C.

CHAPTER 1

Celebrating American Presidents

On the third Monday of February each year, Americans celebrate Presidents' Day. The leader of our country is chosen by the citizens because the United States is a democracy. The president of the United States is one of the most powerful people in the world. Presidents' Day honors American presidents.

Presidents' Day started more than two hundred years ago, but the holiday was not called Presidents' Day. Our country was new, and everyone wanted to honor the first

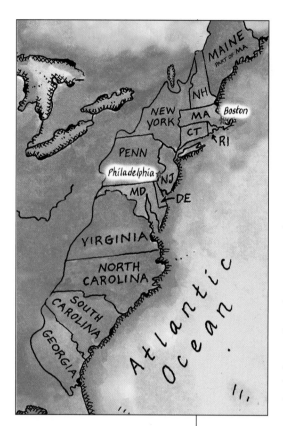

This is a map of the thirteen colonies.

president of the United States, George Washington. He had been a strong leader during the time our nation was forming. He led the American army during the Revolutionary War. The American colonies fought against Great Britain to win their independence. After the Americans won the war, George Washington was elected president. People began to honor Washington by celebrating his birthday.

At the time the United States began, many countries had kings. Someone said that the American president should be called "His Highness the President of the United States of America and Protector of their Liberties." No one liked that idea. Instead of a fancy title, the president is simply called "Mr. President."

The Revolutionary War began with the Battle of Lexington in April, 1775.

The Constitution is a set of laws for the United States. It says that a president is to be elected every four years. At the first election, George Washington got everyone's vote. That never happened again.

By the time Washington was reelected, political parties had formed. People had different ideas about actions the government should take. They joined others with like ideas to form political parties. The political parties

The Constitution is the set of laws for the United States. It starts off with the famous words, "We the people...."

You can see the Constitution at the National Archives Rotunda in Washington, D.C.

each have candidates that run for office. Voters make a choice among these candidates.

As president, George Washington made many decisions about the new country. While Washington was president, the government met in Philadelphia, Pennsylvania. President Washington wanted to find a place to build a permanent capital.

The states of Maryland and Virginia gave the land for the capital. This area is called the District of Columbia. It is not part of any state. In honor of our first president, the city became Washington, D.C.

President Washington asked a Frenchman named Pierre L'Enfant to draw up plans for the capital. L'Enfant was an architect and designer who had served with Washington during the Revolutionary War. L'Enfant had grand ideas for a beautiful city. He chose one hill for the Capitol building and another for the president's home. He made long, extra-wide streets and

Washington, D.C., is made up of land from Maryland and Virginia.

The White House in Washington, D.C. as it looks today.

left space for large government buildings and parks.

George Washington never lived in the new capital. It took ten years to build the city. Even then, it was not complete when President John Adams moved there in 1800.

MISSING PLANS FOR WASHINGTON, D.C.

L'Enfant became angry when people wanted to change some of his plans for Washington, D.C. L'Enfant took his plans and left. Andrew Ellicott and his helper Benjamin Banneker were surveying land for the District of Columbia. They remembered the way L'Enfant laid out the city and were able to complete the project.

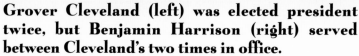

Grover Cleveland (left) was elected president twice, but Benjamin Harrison (right) served between Cleveland's two times in office.

Wagons and ships carried important papers from Philadelphia to Washington, D.C.

Two hundred years later, forty-two men have been president. But there had been forty-three presidencies. Grover Cleveland was president twice, but Benjamin Harrison served between Cleveland's two times in office.

Presidents' Day honors all those who have served as presidents.

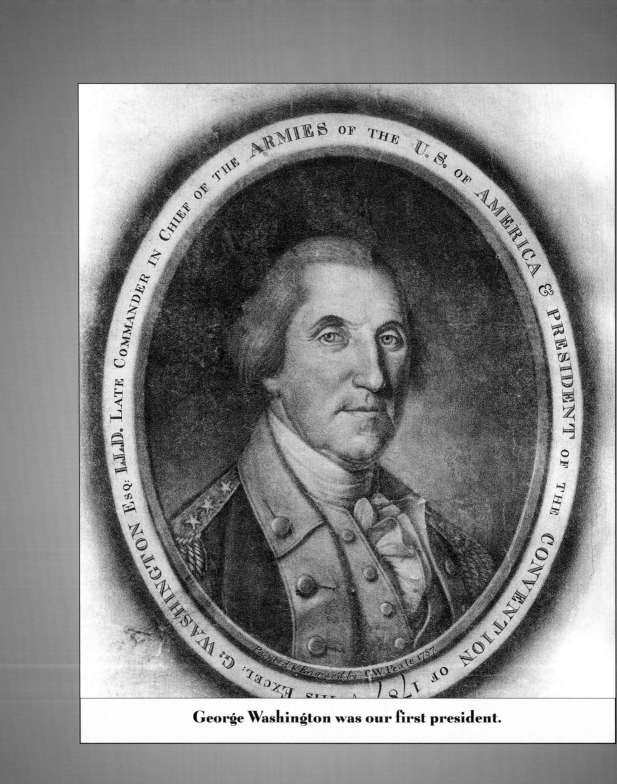

George Washington was our first president.

CHAPTER 2

"The Father of His Country"

George Washington did not plan to be a president. When he was born on February 22, 1732, he was a British citizen. The United States did not exist.

Washington's father owned plantations in Virginia. One of the plantations was on the Potomac River. It was called Mount Vernon. An older stepbrother inherited Mount Vernon when their father died.

By the age of seventeen, Washington was a surveyor. He explored and mapped parts of Virginia where there were no roads or towns. Later, he joined the British army to fight the

GEORGE WASHINGTON

A legend says that young George Washington confessed to his father that he cut down a cherry tree. The story is not true. A minister named Mason Locke Weems made up this story to teach children to be good.

George Washington fought bravely in the French and Indian War.

French, who were fighting the British for control of land in North America.

George Washington was only twenty when his half-brother died. That made him master of Mount Vernon. Washington loved this home on the Potomac River. He made many improvements and experimented with different kinds of crops.

George Washington was a big man. He stood over six feet tall. He had self-control along with good manners. Instead of shaking hands with his guests, he bowed to them. He rarely smiled much because he had trouble with his teeth. Doctors used Washington's own teeth and teeth carved from cow and hippopotamus teeth to make him a set of false teeth. The teeth opened by a metal spring.

Mount Vernon was the family home of George Washington. It is located in Fairfax County, Virginia. Besides being the first president's home, many of his belongings and his grave are there.

Washington

Jacky

Patsy

Martha

George and Martha were married in 1759. George Washington was twenty-six years old when he married Martha Custis.

Washington married Martha Dandridge Custis in 1759. She was a widow with two children. The boy, John Custis, was called Jacky. The girl, named Martha, was called Patsy. Washington sent to England for clothes and books for Jacky. He bought a piano for Patsy.

Washington took part in governing the Virginia colony. The British placed taxes on

Virginia. Washington joined other colonists to protest the taxes.

The first battle of the Revolutionary War took place in 1775 between British troops and Massachusetts colonists. Soon Washington was chosen to lead an army. He was an excellent leader who helped his troops fight and win.

Washington was an excellent leader who inspired his troops.

Washington is inaugurated as first president of the United States.

After the Revolutionary War was over, George Washington was elected president of the United States. He served two terms. Many people wanted him to stay longer, but Washington refused. He felt it was not right for one person to run the country for a long time.

Washington returned to Mount Vernon. Three years later, he became ill and died on

December 14, 1799. He and Martha Washington are buried at Mount Vernon.

During Washington's presidency, several important things happened. The Bill of Rights was adopted. These amendments to the

George Washington was already a national hero by the time he died.

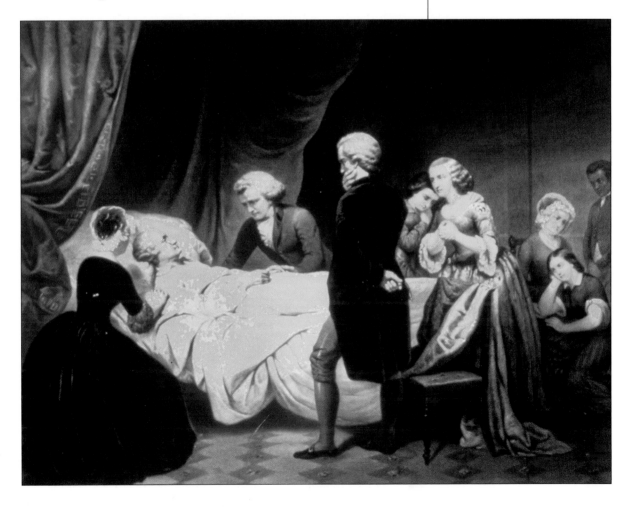

This portrait of George Washington was painted by Gilbert Stuart.

Constitution guarantee personal freedoms for citizens. During his time in office, the Post Office was established. And coins were minted by the government.

George Washington had his portrait painted several times. One of the best-known portraits was done by American painter Gilbert Stuart. Washington posed for the portrait a year before he left the presidency. This picture is on the one-dollar bill.

This is the only photograph ever taken of Abraham Lincoln wearing glasses. Here, he is sitting with his son, Tad.

CHAPTER 3

"Honest Abe"

Abraham Lincoln was six feet four inches tall. Being thin made him seem even taller. He was our tallest president. He began to wear a beard after a little girl suggested that he would look better with one. Lincoln is the one in the top hat.

Nobody would have guessed that Abraham Lincoln would become president when he was born February 12, 1809. His family lived in a log cabin in Kentucky. Lincoln's father was an honest, hardworking man, but they were very poor.

Lincoln's mother did not know how to write her name, but Nancy Hanks Lincoln encouraged her son learn to read. She died when he was nine, and Lincoln's stepmother helped him as well. He went to school for less than a year. Most of what he learned came from reading.

As a young man, Lincoln split logs to make fences.

Lincoln's family moved to Indiana when he was about seven. Lincoln grew tall. He helped his father clear forests and developed muscles splitting logs. He became a very good wrestler. He was known for his honesty. People enjoyed being with him because he told stories and jokes that made them laugh.

When Lincoln was twenty-one years old, the family moved to Illinois. A friend helped him to study law books. Soon Lincoln became a lawyer. People respected him because he carefully prepared his cases.

Abraham Lincoln often borrowed books to read. One of the books he borrowed was Mason Weems's *Life of Washington*.

In 1842, Lincoln married Mary Todd. They had four sons—Robert, Edward (Eddie), William (Willie), and Thomas (Tad).

Lincoln was elected to Congress from Illinois. He spoke strongly against slavery. Later, he ran for the United States Senate.

This is a portrait of the Lincoln family at home in the White House.

In the debates for the Senate, Lincoln made a famous speech stating that "a house divided against itself cannot stand." He felt that slavery was dividing the nation. He wanted to keep the United States together. In a series of debates, he was the better speaker, but he lost the election.

In 1860, the Republican Party had just been organized. The Republican Party chose Abraham Lincoln as its candidate for president. He campaigned against slavery and won the election.

President Lincoln hoped to keep the Union

As a young man, Lincoln made a boat trip to New Orleans. The horror of the slave market turned him against slavery. He said, "As I would not be a slave, so I would not be a master."

together, but several Southern states violently objected to his election. They broke away and formed the Confederate States of America. For the next five years, Americans fought each other in a bitter Civil War.

In 1863, there was a terrible battle at Gettysburg, Pennsylvania. Many soldiers from both sides were killed. President Lincoln went

This map shows what states made up the Confederacy and what states made up the Union.

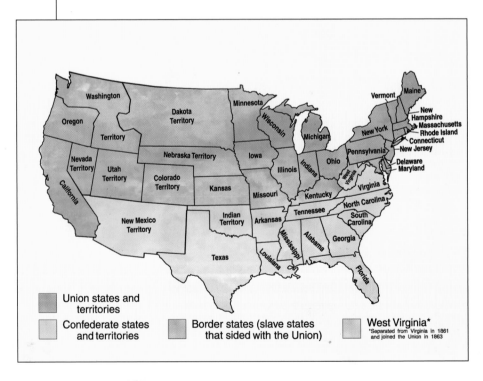

Washington
Oregon
Nevada Territory
California
Utah Territory
Territory
Dakota Territory
Nebraska Territory
Colorado Territory
New Mexico Territory
Kansas
Indian Territory
Texas
Minnesota
Wisconsin
Iowa
Illinois
Missouri
Arkansas
Louisiana
Mississippi
Michigan
Indiana
Ohio
Kentucky
Tennessee
Alabama
Georgia
Florida
Vermont
Maine
New Hampshire
Massachusetts
Rhode Island
Connecticut
New Jersey
Delaware
Maryland
New York
Pennsylvania
West Virginia
Virginia
North Carolina
South Carolina

Union states and territories

Confederate states and territories

Border states (slave states that sided with the Union)

West Virginia*
*Separated from Virginia in 1861 and joined the Union in 1863

The Civil War was the bloodiest war ever fought in America.

to Gettysburg to dedicate the cemetery. People first listened to a two-hour speech by the main speaker. Then Lincoln made a short speech. At Gettysburg, Pennsylvania, Lincoln gave a speech that honored the soldiers who had died for their country. He urged his listeners to preserve the nation so that "government of the people by the people for the people shall not

Today Gettysburg is a national park.

perish from the earth." People clapped politely. Lincoln thought his talk did not go well. Today Lincoln's speech is one of the greatest speeches ever made.

That same year President Lincoln made two important proclamations. One was the Emancipation Proclamation

Abraham Lincoln is known as the Great Emancipator because he worked hard to end slavery.

that freed the slaves. The other was a Thanksgiving Proclamation that set aside a November day to recognize the blessings that our country enjoys.

Lincoln was elected president again in 1864, but he did not serve long. The Civil War ended with the surrender of the Confederacy. A week later, President and Mrs. Lincoln went to Ford's Theater in Washington. As they watched the play, John Wilkes Booth shot the president. Lincoln died the next day, April 15, 1865.

President Lincoln's body was put on a train for a long ride back to Illinois. He was buried in Springfield. Later his wife and three of their children were buried there as well.

Lincoln was the first president to be photographed at his inauguration. But what we remember most about Abraham Lincoln was his honesty, his opposition to slavery, and his efforts to save our nation.

Abraham Lincoln was assassinated while watching a play called *Our American Cousin* at Ford's Theater.

This is the Washington Monument in Washington, D. C.

CHAPTER 4

Presidents and President's Day

Presidents' Day started as a celebration of George Washington's birthday. The first celebration took place during the Revolutionary War even before he became president. General Washington and his troops spent the terrible winter of 1778 at Valley Forge, Pennsylvania. The American soldiers had little to celebrate. The army band cheered everyone up by playing music for Washington's birthday.

Even after Washington was no longer president, people celebrated his birthday. There were dances and parties. In 1885, President Chester Arthur signed a bill that made Washington's

The winter at Valley Forge was cold and harsh.

birthday a holiday for federal employees. By that time, some states were celebrating Abraham Lincoln's birthday as well. That made two holidays in February.

In 1968, Congress passed a law that moved the celebration of Washington's Birthday to the third Monday in February. The Monday holiday gave federal workers a three-day weekend.

Three years later, President Richard Nixon signed a proclamation declaring the third Monday in February to be Presidents' Day. This holiday honored all past presidents, not just Washington and Lincoln.

The people who have served

Chester A. Arthur was president of the United States from 1881 to 1885. He signed a bill in 1885 that made the celebration of Washington's birthday on the third Monday in February.

This is the Lincoln Memorial in Washington, D. C.

as American presidents are as varied as the people who make up our country. Some of the presidents, like George Washington, inherited wealth. Others like Lincoln had to overcome hardships. A number of American presidents served as state governors or members of Congress. Many were lawyers. Some had been soldiers, and several were generals. Others were teachers. Andrew Johnson had been a tailor, and Harry Truman had sold clothing. Ronald Reagan had been a movie actor. Jimmy Carter had been a peanut farmer and later built houses in poor areas after he left office.

Andrew Johnson

Harry Truman

Ronald and Nancy Reagan

Jimmy Carter was state senator, then governor of Georgia, before being elected President.

Americans honor their presidents on Presidents' Day. But they especially remember George Washington and Abraham Lincoln because of their great efforts for our country.

The work of a president has changed since Washington was president but some things stay the same. At Thanksgiving, President George Bush paid a surprise visit to the soldiers serving in the Iraq War.

Presidents' Day Project
★

"If I Were President . . ."

The president of the United States tries to make the country better. Make this booklet to show what you would do if you were president.

You will need:

✔ **3 strips of plain white paper, 8½ inches by 4½ inches**

✔ **pen or pencil**

✔ **ruler**

✔ **scissors**

✔ **stapler**

✔ **red and blue crayons or colored pencils, or patriotic stickers**

1. Stack the 3 strips of paper so that the edges are even.

2. Fold the paper in half, long ends together. (You now have six "pages" 4½ by 4¼ inches.)

3. Use the ruler to measure down 1½ inches from the crease. Draw a thin, straight line across the first page. Cut off the top page at this line.

4. Measure down 2 inches from the crease and draw a line on the second page. Cut off the second page at the line.

42

5. Measure down 2½ inches from the crease, draw a line, and cut the third page.

6. Open the pages to the middle and staple on the crease to keep pages from slipping.

7. Close the pages again. Measure down 3 inches on the fourth page, draw a line, and cut the fourth page.

8. Measure down 3½ inches on the fifth page, draw a line, and cut the fifth page. Do not cut the last page.

9. Close the flip pad. On the top page, write in big letters: "IF I WERE PRESIDENT . . ."

10. On page two, write: "I WOULD . . ."

11. On each of the three blank pages, finish the sentence telling what you would do. Example: Ask everyone to pick up litter.

12. Use a new page for each new idea. Decorate with the colors red, white, and blue, patriotic stickers, or draw your own patriotic symbols.

13. Put your picture on the last page, and sign your name.

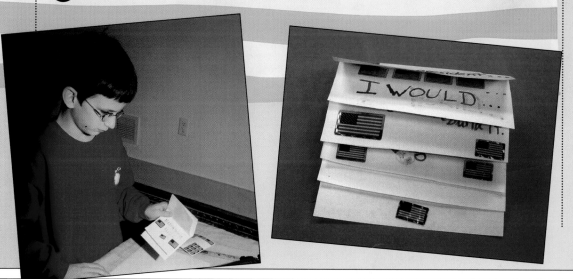

amendments—Changes.

campaign—Making speeches to get votes.

candidate—A person who is running for office.

capital—A city where the government is located.

capitol—The building where members of the government meet.

Civil War—(1860–1865) A war in America between the Northern and Southern states over the issue of slavery; sometimes called the War Between the States.

constitution—Written laws for a country.

debate—Speeches that present both sides of an argument.

Words to Know

★

democracy—A government whose citizens make decisions.

emancipation—The act of setting free.

federal—National.

inauguration—The ceremony of placing an individual in office.

preserve—Keep as is.

proclamation—An official public announcement.

resign—To give up a position.

Revolutionary War—(1776–1781) The war for independence fought by the American colonies against Great Britain.

surveyor—A person who measures land.

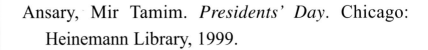 Reading About

Ansary, Mir Tamim. *Presidents' Day*. Chicago: Heinemann Library, 1999.

Freedman, Russell. *Lincoln: A Photobiography*. New York: Houghton Mifflin Co., 1987.

Giblin, James. *George Washington: A Picture Book Biography*. New York: Scholastic Trade, 1998.

Harness, Cheryl. *George Washington.* Washington, D.C.: National Geographic, 2000.

Harness, Cheryl. *Young Abe Lincoln.* Washington, D.C.: National Geographic, 1998.

Nelson, Robin. *Presidents' Day*. Minneapolis, Minn.: Lerner Publications Co., 2002.

Roop, Connie and Peter. *Let's Celebrate Presidents' Day*. Brookfield, Conn.: The Millbrook Press, 2001.

Van Steenwyk, Elizabeth. *When Abraham Talked to the Trees*. Grand Rapids, Mich.: Eerdmans Books for Young Readers, 2000.

Internet Addresses

★

U.S. PRESIDENTS—UNITED IN SERVICE
<http://www.whitehouse.gov/kids/presidents/
index.html>

INSIDE THE WHITE HOUSE
*Pretend that you have been elected the president
of the United States. What would you do?*
<http://www.nationalgeographic.com/
features/96/whitehouse/whhome.html>

Index